MW01001689

AN IDEAS INTO ACTION GUIDEBOOK

Changing Yourself and Your Reputation

IDEAS INTO ACTION GUIDEBOOKS

Aimed at managers and executives who are concerned with their own and others' development, each guidebook in this series gives specific advice on how to complete a developmental task or solve a leadership problem.

LEAD CONTRIBUTOR	Talula Cartwright
CONTRIBUTORS	Bill Adams, Corey Criswell, Michelle Crouch, Kelly Hannum, Cindy McLaughlin, Bertrand Sereno, Stephanie Trovas, Hughes Van Stichel, Jeffrey Yip
DIRECTOR OF ASSESSMENT, TOOLS, AND PUBLICATIONS	Sylvester Taylor
EDITOR	Peter Scisco
ASSOCIATE EDITOR	Karen Lewis
DESIGN AND LAYOUT	Joanne Ferguson, Clinton Press
CONTRIBUTING ARTISTS	Laura J. Gibson
	Chris Wilson, 29 & Company

Copyright ©2009 Center for Creative Leadership.

All Rights Reserved. No part of this publication may be reproduced, stored in a retrieval system, or transmitted, in any form or by any means, electronic, mechanical, photocopying, recording, or otherwise, without the prior written permission of the publisher. Printed in the United States of America.

CCL No. 445
ISBN No. 978-1-60491-069-8

CENTER FOR CREATIVE LEADERSHIP
POST OFFICE BOX 26300
GREENSBORO, NORTH CAROLINA 27438-6300
336-288-7210
WWW.CCL.ORG / PUBLICATIONS

AN IDEAS INTO ACTION GUIDEBOOK

Changing Yourself and Your Reputation

Talula Cartwright

Center for
Creative
Leadership

www.ccl.org

THE IDEAS INTO ACTION GUIDEBOOK SERIES

This series of guidebooks draws on the practical knowledge that the Center for Creative Leadership (CCL®) has generated, since its inception in 1970, through its research and educational activity conducted in partnership with hundreds of thousands of managers and executives. Much of this knowledge is shared—in a way that is distinct from the typical university department, professional association, or consultancy. CCL is not simply a collection of individual experts, although the individual credentials of its staff are impressive; rather it is a community, with its members holding certain principles in common and working together to understand and generate practical responses to today's leadership and organizational challenges.

The purpose of the series is to provide managers with specific advice on how to complete a developmental task or solve a leadership challenge. In doing that, the series carries out CCL's mission to advance the understanding, practice, and development of leadership for the benefit of society worldwide. We think you will find the Ideas Into Action Guidebooks an important addition to your leadership toolkit.

Table of Contents

EXECUTIVE BRIEF

This book offers help in making changes—and in getting people to notice them. Changing is hard work. One part of that work is the change itself. You must decide to change and then make the change happen. That in itself is a big accomplishment. But what if you're doing all that work and making significant changes—and no one notices? It can be very discouraging! But take heart! This book shows you how to move on with the second part of the work, the follow-through: getting people to notice that you are changing.

A Two-Part Process

Changing is hard work. One part of that work is the change itself. You must decide to change and then make the change happen. That in itself is a big accomplishment. But what if you're doing all that work and making significant changes—and no one notices? It can be very discouraging! Then it's time for the second part, the follow-through: getting people to notice that you are changing. Read on for help in making changes—and in getting people to notice them.

The Challenge of Personal Change

In order to change, you have to first decide for yourself that you need to change. Change is always a choice, of course. You could remain just as you are. Stability is easier than progress, and you certainly wouldn't want to get worse! Since you have the freedom of choice, you also have the responsibility to choose well. The old way is always more familiar, and it creates a kind of default setting that is all too easy to snap back into. It takes work to make a real change.

To develop your capacity to lead, you must start with an assessment of your strengths and weaknesses. In other words, to get where you want to go, you need to know where you are. Then you will be ready to create a plan to optimize and leverage your strengths and to work on developing better skills in other areas.

As you create your plan, you may notice a curious paradox: Often your strengths and weaknesses relate to the same quality. If you are known for your flexibility, for example, you may also get feedback that you are indecisive. If you work to alleviate your indecisive behaviors, you may inadvertently diminish the favorable view that flexibility is one of your strengths. Any developmental plan of action you take should not only improve a weakness but also maintain a strength. If the change to the new desired behavior is too drastic, it is actually possible to damage people's perception of a strength—to sacrifice it on the altar of improved performance!

Working on a personal quality presents specific challenges. The fact is that most personal qualities in and of themselves are neither strengths nor weaknesses. It's the context in which you practice your leadership that often creates in the minds of others a judgment of whether a specific quality is good or bad. In one work environment it may pay for a leader to be more flexible—for

360-Degree Assessments

Effectiveness is judged differently in different environments. A good assessment is key to inform you of how you are being judged. It lets you know whether you need to change yourself, change the way you present yourself, or do a bit of both. You may find one of the following CCL assessments helpful.

Executive Dimensions assesses top-level leadership behaviors. A straightforward feedback report displays a participant's data grouped into three factors: leading the business, leading others, and leading by personal example. These factors are further divided into sixteen competencies, containing a total of ninety-two items.

Benchmarks assesses sixteen skills and perspectives that CCL researchers have identified as critical to successful management. In addition, it helps you identify five potential flaws that may stall or derail a promising career.

Prospector assesses the leadership skills most often found in successful executives and the learning behaviors needed to acquire those skills.

360 by Design assesses any of CCL's ninety-four research-grounded competencies and five derailment factors. The instrument can be customized to address the behaviors and skills important to high performance in your organization. It can be short or long, focused or general.

Skillscope assesses fifteen key job-related skills essential for managerial success.

For more information about these assessments, please visit www.ccl.org.

example, during the early stages of product development when innovative ideas need to be encouraged and solicited. In a different case, the quality of decisiveness may be more highly valued—for example, when dealing with the publicity surrounding a crisis in your organization. In such an environment, a leader would need to react smoothly to rapidly changing circumstances. It would be essential for the leader to be more decisive, so flexibility could actually undermine effectiveness.

The goal that you set for yourself in your development plan must reflect this challenge of altering what might be considered a personality trait in order to improve your effectiveness. And since what you are really trying to alter is not only your effectiveness but also people's judgment of it, it also requires some public relations.

The Challenge of Conflicting Commitments

A conflicting commitment poses a significant challenge to achieving any goal, and especially when that goal is a change in behavior. It's important that you figure out a way to honor any strong commitment that might compete with your goal. Consider, for example, an executive who wants to lose weight but finds that the goal conflicts with his desire to give his family, his employees, and himself "the very best." His desire to be magnanimous often expresses itself in lavish dinners. He has to become aware of this rival goal before he can honor it in a different way and still reach his personal goal of losing weight.

Another example is a manager who sets a goal of being a better listener and who has a reputation of being very efficient. She might see the need to spend time listening as interfering with her performance, which would compromise a reputation that she highly values. She has to come to terms with both of these impulses. She can successfully change when she no longer sees these personal desires as conflicting, as an either-or choice.

Making Changes

Before anyone can recognize the changes you have made, you have to actually change, of course. This may involve working on habitual behaviors—those that have developed to a stage where they have become automatic—you don't even think about them. To change such behaviors, you have to make yourself conscious of them and bring them back into your active thought process. It can be frustrating at first, but it's necessary. Consider the model below.

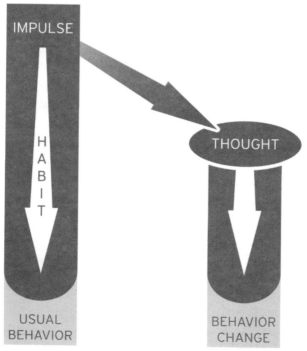

IMPULSE

HABIT

USUAL BEHAVIOR

THOUGHT

BEHAVIOR CHANGE

When you identify an impulse, such as blurting out a response before someone else has finished speaking, it allows you to think before you act and to change your behavior.

Many people eat, drink, or smoke, for example, without thinking about it. The impulse simply results in a habitual action: getting a snack, pouring a drink, lighting a cigarette. As soon as the impulse is identified, a thought has been engaged, and it is possible to change the behavior. With conscious effort, a person can close the refrigerator door, put the bottle back, or put out the cigarette.

Here Be Dragons

Legend has it that on some ancient maps you can find the letters *H.B.D.* inscribed at the edge where the uncharted waters begin. The letters stand for "Here Be Dragons" and warn that there may be dangerous creatures in the unexplored territories. Even though this legend may not be factual, there is some truth related to it. Unexplored territory can be scary. Anytime you move from an old way of doing things to a new way, it generates a certain amount of discomfort. Going into this new territory and engaging in unfamiliar practices can make you feel lost and unsure of yourself. What can you do when you confront one of these dragons in the uncharted waters of your leadership? You can seek refuge in the harbor of your old habits. That will give you shelter and comfort, but it will deny you the success you will experience if you stay on course. The feedback and support you get from others can help you navigate this unfamiliar territory.

Perception Is Everything

Once you have set a goal and started working on it, you're faced with a problem: How do you get people to notice that you are changing? People tend to see others through the same lens or set of expectations they have always used. It's not easy for them to take a different perspective. You have probably heard stories about women who dye their hair and their husbands don't notice, or men who shave off their beards and it goes unremarked. Maybe you have had such an experience yourself.

Imagine how much harder it is for people to notice when you make a much more subtle change, such as practicing patience or listening more attentively. If you have set a goal to be more decisive but people continue to think of you as indecisive, how do you get them to notice that you're changing?

It's possible not only to respond to people's perceptions but also to lead those perceptions. For example, you can make a public announcement of your goals. Point out to people that you are making changes to your behavior, and use specific phrases that call attention to your actions. For example, you might say, "I've received some feedback about my being indecisive, so I'm going to make a decision here." Or you might make a specific reference to your development plan: "I'm working on a goal of making decisions more quickly, so let's see how I do here."

Not only do such announcements mark the intended change for others, but they also invite feedback and assessment, which are essential to your development. In order to develop, you have to change, but you must also advertise and market your changes. Use the Behavior Change Worksheet on page 17 to think through the approach you want to take and to think about the support

Go Public

- Ask at least one person to help you with your goals.
- Take at least two actions to support your goals.
- Set up a meeting to share your goals with your boss, your group, your peers, or your direct reports.
- Practice new behaviors.
- Choose the goals you want to get feedback on, and decide how you want to get that information.
- Select feedback partners you trust.
- Ask your feedback partners whether they see a change.
- Focus on results.
- Keep a journal of your activities, the results, and the feedback you receive.

resources you want to have in place. You can review a sample of the worksheet on page 16.

People often see you through the same lens they have always used because it makes their interactions with you easier. We all store away a certain number of expectations about another person's behavior. Small, incremental changes that you make in your leadership style or communication skills are often lost on a busy and preoccupied audience, but there are things you can do to help people notice.

How to Get Noticed

Changing ineffective habits takes work. Before you can even tackle the problem of making a change, you have to decide to change. After you make a change, you have to have patience and a strategy for getting people to notice that you are changing. You can shape that strategy with tactics that involve feedback, coaching, and other developmental relationships. Approach change honestly, reach out to others, persevere through the transition from old behavior to new, and partner with others who will give you constructive feedback on your actions.

Receiving and Responding to Feedback

When you receive feedback, treat it as an important gift. You can measure its importance partly by how much it helps you increase your awareness about your actions and how they affect others. If you learn from feedback something about yourself that you didn't know before, or you learn something about the impact you have on others that you didn't realize before, then you have received a very important gift—one that isn't easy to come by.

If you think of feedback as a gift, you will want to recognize it and thank the person who has given it to you. You can construct your appreciation as an opportunity to further publicize and market the changes you are making so that you can continue to receive constructive feedback and assessments.

For example, you could gather the people who have responded to a written assessment of you, such as a 360-degree developmental evaluation, and tell them something like this:

I appreciate the feedback you have given me. You told me I am doing well getting and disseminating information, and I am glad to know that. I realize that being an effective conduit for information is an essential part of my role as a manager in this organization. You also told me I could do some work on being more emotionally accessible, and I am committed to doing that.

I need your suggestions on how to achieve this. I am going to leave the room so that you can talk freely, and I ask that one of you

Behavior Change Worksheet: Sample

What feedback have you received?

People view me as indecisive.

Which of your personality traits or preferences does the feedback relate to?

Preference for intuitive perceiving on MBTI, preference for originator on CSI, preference for innovator/visionary on CPI.

What related strength do you want to maintain?

flexibility, creativity

What change in your behavior would be useful?

I always wait until the last minute to announce a decision in case a "better deal" comes along or in case I get new information. I could use my strength of flexibility and not do this every time. Sometimes I could announce a decision early, since I know this is something people need from me.

How could you "market" this change?

I could let people know my preference to announce a decision late, and why I prefer that, when I announce something early, so they will know I am changing my behavior.

Who are possible feedback partners?

my peers and my family members

Behavior Change Worksheet

What feedback have you received?

_____

Which of your personality traits or preferences does the feedback relate to?

_____

_____

_____

What related strength do you want to maintain?

_____

What change in your behavior would be useful?

_____

_____

_____

_____

How could you "market" this change?

_____

_____

_____

Who are possible feedback partners?

_____

write the group's suggestions on this flipchart. I want you to know that I am really going to give it my best effort because it is important to me. I'll come back to the room in thirty minutes and read your suggestions. You can just leave them on the chart for me, or if you want to, you're welcome to stick around and talk about it or come to me later.

Another approach would be to send your 360-degree assessment respondents a letter similar to the sample below:

Dear [Respondent's Name],

Thank you for supporting my development as a leader by responding to the 360-degree assessment in advance of my leadership development program. I know this was an imposition on your time, and I sincerely appreciate your support in my continuing development.

I want my journey of development to continue beyond the formal leadership development program I attended. Coming out of the course, I have identified the following strengths and developmental needs:

<u>Strengths</u>
Resourcefulness and decisiveness
Organization and attention to detail
Being a quick study

<u>Developmental Needs</u>
Self-awareness
Building and mending relationships

I am asking for your support again by providing me feedback on any or all of these areas in the coming weeks and months. If you see me exhibiting behaviors that should be reinforced or behaviors

A Key Ingredient

Marshall Goldsmith, in *The Art and Practice of Leadership Coaching,* says he resists taking someone on as a coaching client if key people (such as the potential client's boss) won't agree to provide feedback during the process. Many executive coaches follow a similar practice, which underscores the importance of feedback during any endeavor to make personal changes.

that need improvement, I ask that you pull me aside and tell me what you observed and the impact it had on you. I will endeavor to accept all such feedback as it is offered—that is, for my development as a leader within this organization.

Thank you for your continuing support.

With warmest regards,
[Your Name]

Enrolling a Coach

One way to make it more likely that people will notice your changes is to give them a stake in the outcome. You can do this by asking them to coach you on the goal. Think of this *not* as a professional coaching role, but as an informal one—more of a learning partner than an executive coach. If you're working to change a specific behavior that a person has given you feedback on, you might enlist some coaching support using this or a similar approach:

Thank you for your feedback on my recent development assessment. I learned that I may have some work to do in the area of being a good listener, and I want you to know that I am committed to doing that work. Would you be willing to give me feedback when you think I'm doing a good job of listening to you? And would you also be willing to take me aside and let me know privately when you think I'm not doing a good job of listening to you—or someone else, if you happen to witness it?

With this kind of an approach, you establish a connection with an informal coach. This approach pays double dividends: you have given your coach a stake in helping you achieve your goal (building support that will help you make changes), and you have also encouraged that person to change his or her perception of you (publicizing the change you are making).

It's important that you insist on feedback from your coach because it also helps him or her to notice when you are doing things differently. The coach you have recruited will watch for you to make the changes he or she has recommended. It's as important for you to be told when you are doing it right (reaching the goal) as it is when you are doing it wrong. A sense of success is a real boost to your morale and an incentive to continue and to practice new behavior. Your coach's feedback provides an immediate and accurate view of what your new actions mean to others.

Follow up with your coach after a short while. Schedule a time to sit down with him or her and ask for feedback. Accept the feedback graciously, regardless of how clumsily or elegantly it may be delivered. It is to your benefit to keep this coach. The best way to accept this gift of feedback is to simply say thank you and ask for more. When your coach has exhausted the store of feedback he or she has for you, then say something like this:

I really appreciate this coaching. It means a lot to me, and I'll be happy to return the favor any time you ask. It's a very useful way for me to learn. Would you be willing to continue our coaching relationship just a bit longer?

If your coach agrees, then say something like this:

> *What do you think is the one most important thing I can concentrate on for the next month or so to continue working on my listening skills?*

End with the feedback-contracting questions again (asking for feedback when you're doing a good job, and when you're not), and you have another informal coaching contract. If your coach hesitates or doesn't agree to continue, don't worry. You can simply move on to someone else.

Building Other Developmental Relationships

A developmental relationship is a relationship in a work setting that is particularly developmental—that is, a relationship that is a key source of assessment, challenge, and support. A relationship with an informal coach as described above is, of course, one such relationship. Other developmental relationships may include those with a mentor, a boss, a colleague, a spouse. Any developmental relationship provides some mixture of the following roles:

- A *feedback provider* can give you ongoing feedback as you work to learn and improve.

- A *sounding board* can help you evaluate strategies before you implement them.

- A *feedback interpreter* can help you integrate or make sense of the feedback you get from others.

- A *dialogue partner* provides perspectives or points of view that are different from your own.

- An *assignment broker* gives you access to challenging assignments, such as a new job or additions to your current one.

- An *accountability partner* puts pressure on you to fulfill your commitment to your goal.

- A *role model* serves as an example of high (or low) competence in the area you're developing.

- A *counselor* can help you determine what is making learning and development difficult.

- A *cheerleader* helps boost your belief that success is possible.

- A *positive reinforcer* provides formal rewards for your progress toward your goal.

- A *companion* gives you the sense that you are not alone in your struggles.

It's not likely that one person can play all of the roles needed for your development. Figure out which roles are needed, and find the right people for those roles. Remember that the people who play one or more of these roles will have a stake in helping you achieve your goal. This makes it more likely that you will be successful—and that they will notice your success and change their perceptions of you.

Assembling a Group

Sometimes you are able to enroll an entire group of potential learning partners by meeting with your 360-degree assessment respondents or some other group. If they feel comfortable with your asking them for feedback without your leaving the room, they may be able to suggest something that they can do to help you, such as giving you a sign during meetings. Or they may just agree to give you feedback through a more formal arrangement, like another assessment sometime in the future, which you could use to see what kind of progress you are making. You could develop a less formal assessment yourself that would ask for feedback on a specific goal after a reasonable amount of time. Asking for feedback requires a willingness to be vulnerable, but it models something very important to your group members—the need for openness and communication. And if communication within your group is already good, they will probably respond positively.

Once you've done this, you will have enrolled an entire group of potential coaches and called their attention to the changes you are making. You may get a growing list of helpful ideas that will tell you more specifically what they meant by their general feedback.

Reaching Out

To recruit allies in your campaign to change yourself and to get your changes noticed, you may need to reach out. There may be folks you have offended, and you may need to apologize. You may need to offer a smile, a greeting, or a friendly handshake to get people to notice you again so they can start processing the "new you." Don't neglect this. When you are respectful and friendly, it's easier for people to start noticing that you're different.

It may help people take a new look at you if you make an obvious visible change. Depending on what you are working on, this may mean getting to work a little earlier, walking a different path through the office building, going to meetings you've been skipping, or dropping by to visit and chat. If you are working on being more approachable, for example, you can change your office setup or the way you dress. The key is to do something visibly different that relates to the less visible behavior change.

Changing ineffective habits—of thought or behavior—takes work. Part of that work is the change itself. You must decide to change and then make the change happen. Another important part of change lies in getting people to notice that you are changing. That requires patience, good marketing, honesty, reaching out to others, perseverance to get through the transition, and partnerships with others who will give you good feedback along the way.

Suggested Readings

Bridges, W. (2003). *Managing transitions: Making the most of change* (2nd ed.). Cambridge, MA: Da Capo Press.

Browning, H., & Van Velsor, E. (2001). *Three keys to development: Defining and meeting your leadership challenges* (Rev. ed.). Greensboro, NC: Center for Creative Leadership.

Cartwright, T. (2007). *Setting priorities: Personal values, organizational results.* Greensboro, NC: Center for Creative Leadership.

Fleenor, J. W., Taylor, S., & Chappelow, C. (2008). *Leveraging the impact of 360-degree feedback.* San Francisco: Pfeiffer.

Hernez-Broome, G., McLaughlin, C., & Trovas, S. (2006). *Selling yourself without selling out: A leader's guide to ethical self-promotion.* Greensboro, NC: Center for Creative Leadership.

Kirkland, K., & Manoogian, S. (1998). *Ongoing feedback: How to get it, how to use it.* Greensboro, NC: Center for Creative Leadership.

Morgan, H., Harkins, P., & Goldsmith, M. (2005). *The art and practice of leadership coaching: 50 top executive coaches reveal their secrets.* Hoboken, NJ: Wiley.

Riddle, D. (2008). *Leadership coaching: When it's right and when you're ready.* Greensboro, NC: Center for Creative Leadership.

Background

The advice given in this guidebook is drawn from CCL's ongoing research into how individuals set and achieve leadership goals, as well as our educational experience with participants in CCL programs. We concentrate on goal setting and action planning at the end of our programs, and we follow up with participants about their success in achieving their goals. Are they able to see the positive changes they are making? Do their observers—their bosses, superiors, direct reports, peers, and others—notice that they are changing? One thing we have learned is that people find it discouraging when they do the work of changing themselves—but no one notices the change. This guidebook addresses that problem and offers help in solving it.

Key Point Summary

Changing is hard work. Part of that work is the change itself. You must decide to change and then make the change happen. Another important part is the follow-through: getting people to notice that you are changing.

Start by assessing your strengths and weaknesses. You may notice that they relate to the same quality. In that case, try to improve the weakness while maintaining the strength. You may have another commitment that conflicts with your goal. If so, figure out a way to honor that commitment. You can successfully change when you no longer see the two as an either-or choice. You may have to work on a habitual behavior—one that has become automatic. To change such a behavior, you have to make yourself conscious of it and bring it back into your active thought process. Then you can identify the impulse, think before you act, and change the behavior.

Once you have set a goal and started working on it, you need to get people to notice that you are changing. You can lead their perceptions by making a public announcement of your goal. Doing so marks the intended change for others, and it also invites feedback and assessment, which are essential to your development.

Other tactics involve feedback, coaching, and other developmental relationships. When you receive feedback, thank the person who has given it to you. Expressing your appreciation is an opportunity to publicize the changes you are making. You can also help people notice your changes by giving them a stake in the outcome. You can do this by asking them to coach you on the goal. Other developmental relationships include those with a mentor, a boss, a colleague, or a spouse. Such relationships help by building support that helps you make changes and by publicizing the changes you are making.

Ordering Information

TO GET MORE INFORMATION, TO ORDER OTHER IDEAS INTO ACTION GUIDEBOOKS, OR TO FIND OUT ABOUT BULK-ORDER DISCOUNTS, PLEASE CONTACT US BY PHONE AT 336-545-2810 OR VISIT OUR ONLINE BOOKSTORE AT WWW.CCL.ORG/GUIDEBOOKS.

NEW *from the* **Center for Creative Leadership**

Transforming Your Leadership Culture

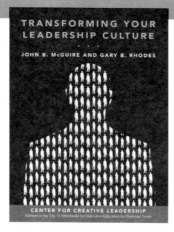

Imagine the power of leadership as a unified force for adaptable, sustainable organizational change, and you can see why we say, "Change the leadership culture and you change the organizational culture."

Transforming Your Leadership Culture is first and foremost for executives and organizational leaders who see that change is necessary but are skeptical that lasting, sustainable change–transformation–lies within their reach. When leaders take on and follow through on cultural transformation alongside their strategic and operational changes, they consistently succeed in terms of performance goals–while other organizations fail to change and struggle to survive. Think of this book as your survival guide to leading change.

STOCK NO. **2289**   PRICE **$42**

Center for Creative Leadership

www.ccl.org

To order your copy, visit **www.ccl.org/tylc**.